Software Solutions

INTRODUCTION

TO

4D SUITE

Jeanne Styles

VSM 360000086

ACKNOWLEDGEMENTS

Thanks to my husband, Ben, who has patiently supported me throughout the process of writing this book. His faithful encouragement has been a blessing.

Thanks to my parents and owners of Creative Sewing, Bob and Linda Christian, whose passion for serving others through their business serves as the inspiration for this book. Their long-term experience as local Pfaff dealers has been an invaluable asset.

Thanks to my sister, Carol Joiner, who is more than a sister—she is a best friend. She has shared her wealth of experience in the business of sewing.

Thanks to those who have attended my 4D software training classes and have offered suggestions for additions or improvements to the material in this book.

Thanks to the team at Pfaff and VSM software who design creative and forward-looking products for the software and embroidery market.

With gratitude to each of you,
Jeanne Styles

ABOUT THE AUTHOR

Jeanne Styles is the author of the Software Solutions 4D Embroidery software workbook series. Her experience in software engineering, secondary education, embroidery, and freelance writing provides a unique background for these workbooks.

Jeanne received her undergraduate degree from the University of Alabama before beginning work as a software systems engineer. After her husband completed a master's degree, his job relocation opened the door for Jeanne to accept a position teaching high school science and math while continuing her own graduate studies in secondary education. Ben, Jeanne, and their two sons now reside near her parents, Bob and Linda Christian, owners of Creative Sewing in Huntsville, Alabama. Jeanne teaches 4D Embroidery software classes at their store and is currently pursuing opportunities in freelance writing. To contact her, visit www.learn4D.com

INTRODUCTION

Background Information 2
Install 4D Suite...3
Install Additional Images 4
Smart Update...4

DESIGN CREATOR

Introduction 5
Exercise 1: "Double Loops" 6
   Create Express Embroidery...6
   Edit, Create, and Picture Tabs...8
   Select Work Area..8
   Change Fill Properties 9
   Convert to Stipple Fill..10
   Save Design 12

Exercise 2: "Santa Hat" 14
   Load Picture 14
   QuickStitch Fill Hat 15
   Add Ripple Pattern Fill to Hat Rim 17
   Add Motif Fill to Hat Tassel..18
   Add Border 19
   Save .can and .vp3 Files 20

Additional Features 20

4D CROSS STITCHER

Introduction 23
Exercise 1: "Floral Frame"...24
   Create QuickCross Design 24
   Remove Background Crosses 26
   Add TrueType Font..27
   Generate Stitches and Save Files......................................30

Additional Features 31

4D STITCH EDITOR

Introduction 32
Exercise 1: "Star Quilt Block"....................................32
    Express Create a Quilt Block Design 32
    Open Design in 4D Stitch Editor 35
    Remove Stitch Points 35
    Add Stamp Fill 36
    Add Second Stamp Fill 37
    Add Border 37
    Global Morphing 39
    Point Morphing 40

Additional Features 42

4D SKETCH

Introduction 43
Install Pen Tablet and ArtRage...............................43
Using A Pen Tablet 44
    Pen Tablet Conventions 45

ArtRage...46
Printable Fabrics 47
Design and Alignment Options 48
    Design Wizard Options 48
    Alignment Options 48

4D Sketch Exercise 1: "3D Flower"..........................49
    Load Flower Picture..49
    Free Motion Thread Painting 50
    Quilt Motion 51
    Rotational Zig-Zag 52
    Motif Motion..53

Additional Features 54
Ideas 56

4D PICTURE STITCH

Introduction 57
Exercise 1: "Woman's Face" 59
    Load Picture 59
    Set Stitch Options...60
    Convert to Black and White and Crop..............61
    Alter Facial Contrast 62
    Add Facial Highlights 62
    Remove Unnecessary Stitches..........................64

Additional Features 65
Design Suggestions 66

4D FABRIC DECORATOR

Introduction 67
Exercise 1: "Gold Lace"...67
    Launch Motif Wizard...67
    Combine Two Motifs 68
    Save .can and Embroidery Files 69

Exercise 2: "Floating Hearts"...............................70
    Select Picture for New Motif..............................70
    Add Candlewicking Stitch 71
    Create Fabric..72

Additional Features 74

4D STITCH ARTIST

Introduction 75
Exercise 1: "Crescent" Maxi Stitch......................75
    Create Maxi Stitch 75
    View Stitch in 3D and Real Size 77
    Alter Stitch Color..77

Additional Features 77

4D DESIGN ALIGNER

Introduction 78
Exercise 1: Split a Large Flower 78
   Open Design 78
   Prepare to Split Design..78
   Split Design into Sections 80
   Preview and Print Sections 80
How to Stitch a Split Design 81
Where to Split a Design...81

4D FONT DIGITIZING

Introduction 82

TEACHER'S GUIDE

Recommended Classroom Supplies 86
Recommended Teacher Preparation.....................................86
Suggested Class Schedules...87

INTRODUCTION

Technology has opened an amazing world of creativity to both the home and the professional machine embroidery markets today. An embroidery machine combined with quality embroidery software provides the tools for creating custom embroidered projects. Your imagination opens the door to this exciting new art form. Would you like to create a beautiful heirloom embroidered photo, a hand cross-stitch without the handwork, or a thread painting with the ease of drawing with pen and paper? Perhaps you envision a new patchwork stitch or an embroidered quilt. The 4D Embroidery Suite software accords these and many more creative possibilities.

As the innovation of embroidery software increases, so do both the complexity and the simplicity. This may seem like a paradox, but the beauty of the 4D Embroidery Suite software is that in spite of its robust design, this generation of software is even easier to use than its predecessor, 3D Embroidery Suite.

The purpose of this book, then, is to provide simple, fun exercises that demonstrate foundational 4D Suite techniques—to give you the tools to fulfill your passion to fashion artful embroidery.

This is the second book in the *Software Solutions: 4D Embroidery* series. It introduces the following 4D Embroidery software modules: 4D Design Creator, 4D Cross Stitcher, 4D Stitch Editor, 4D Sketch, 4D Picture Stitch, 4D Fabric Decorator, 4D Stitch Artist, 4D Design Aligner, and 4D Font Digitizing.

The first book in this series, *Software Solutions: 4D Embroidery Extra*, covered the modules included in 4D Extra: 4D Configure, 4D File Assistant, 4D Organizer, 4D Embroidery Extra (also referred to as 4D Extra), and 4D Vision. Since these modules are also part of the 4D Suite software package, it is helpful, though not essential, to complete the exercises in the first book before proceeding to this book.

BACKGROUND INFORMATION

Before beginning the exercises in this book, it is helpful to understand how to use these features in 4D Embroidery Extra:

- Transfer a design from the computer to the embroidery machine using Send1 **1** or Send2 **2**.
- Cut and paste portions of a design using the Edit tab.
- Create a simple design using the Express Design Wizard.
- Add text and create a new font under the Letters tab.

If you need to review these foundational techniques and concepts, refer to one of these three reference materials:

1. *Software Solutions: 4D Embroidery Extra* **Workbook**
   The 4D Organizer and 4D File Assistant chapters explain how to send a design to the embroidery machine. In the 4D Embroidery Extra chapter, refer to Exercises 1 and 2 to review lettering and fonts, Exercise 3 to review editing, and Exercises 4-6 to review the Express Design Wizard.

2. **4D Extra Tutorials**
   To access the interactive software tutorials, choose Start→All Programs→4D Embroidery System→Learning Center. Select the 4D Embroidery Extra tutorial program.

3. **4D Embroidery Extra Reference Guides**
   Choose Start→All Programs→4D Embroidery System→ Reference Guides→Main Modules. Double click on *4DEmbroideryReferenceGuide.pdf* to open it. The Adobe PDF Reference Guides contain the same information as the printed manuals included inside the 4D Suite box.

   Customers who received a free upgrade from 3D Suite to 4D Suite did not receive printed manuals. These customers may wish to order a manual kit from their local Pfaff dealership. The kit includes a printed set of the program manuals and a bonus CD containing thousands of clip-art images designed for use with the 4D Suite software. Some workbook exercises use images from the Picture Library folder of this CD.

If you have not already installed 4D Suite, insert the 4D dongle into a USB port and place the 4D Suite program DVD into the computer's DVD drive. Most people will need to complete a four-step process to install the program.

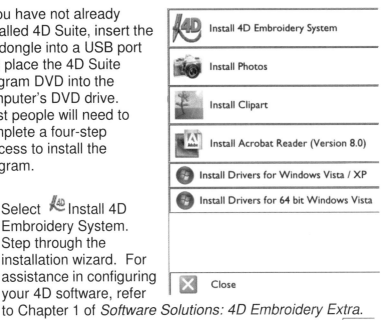

1. Select Install 4D Embroidery System. Step through the installation wizard. For assistance in configuring your 4D software, refer to Chapter 1 of *Software Solutions: 4D Embroidery Extra.*

2. Return to the installation menu. Select Install Photos ![camera icon]. Follow the instructions given.

3. Return to the installation menu and select Install Clipart ![clipart icon]. Follow the instructions given.

4. Return to the installation menu. Install only one of the drivers. Most people should select Install Drivers for Windows Vista / XP.

It is typically unnecessary to install the Adobe Acrobat Reader since this program comes pre-installed on most computers. After completing the steps listed above, Close the installation menu. Remember to remove the DVD from the computer. Carefully guard these three items: the 4D Suite installation DVD, the Product License Code and the 4D Suite dongle. The dongle must be connected to a powered USB port anytime you use the software.

INSTALL ADDITIONAL IMAGES

The 4D Suite box includes a CD entitled, *ClipArt, Photos, and Bonus Designs*. Some of the exercises in this book utilize images from this CD.

Customers who received a free upgrade from 3D Suite to 4D Suite (those who purchased 3D Suite immediately before 4D Suite was released), did not receive printed manuals or this CD. To obtain these images, order a manual kit from your local Pfaff dealer. The kit includes printed software manuals and a CD containing thousands of clip-art images designed for use with the 4D Suite software.

1. Insert the CD into the CD or DVD drive to launch the installation menu. Choose Install 4D Bonus Designs and step through the installation wizard.
2. Return to the menu and install the photos.
3. Return to the menu and install the clipart images.

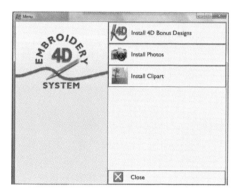

SMART UPDATE

It is important to check regularly for 4D Embroidery program updates. Open 4D Configure . Connect to the internet and select Smart Update. Follow the instructions to update the software.

INTRODUCTION

4D Design Creator ⚜ automatically converts a digital image file, such as a piece of clip art or a logo, into an embroidery design. (Always obtain permission for copyrighted images.) In this exercise, you will convert a clip-art image into an embroidery design and then customize the new design. 4D Design Creator is similar to the Express Design Wizard in 4D Extra, but offers many expanded features to customize the automatically prepared design. 4D Design Creator also includes tools to digitize a design from scratch.

Launch 4D Design Creator from 4D Extra (or any of the other 4D Software modules) by selecting the 4D Design Creator icon ⚜ from the top toolbar.

Both exercises in this chapter use an image from the Picture Library folder found on the bonus clipart CD. Those who do not own this CD may follow the techniques demonstrated in the primary exercises with a suggested alternate image.

CREATE EXPRESS EMBROIDERY

1. Open 4D Embroidery Extra by selecting Start→All Programs→4D Embroidery System→4D Embroidery Extra.

2. Start 4D Design Creator by clicking on the 4D Design Creator icon (located on the top toolbar).

3. Select Cancel. Choose Preferences  from the top toolbar. Under the Screen tab, ensure that the Color Tolerance box is unchecked (open). OK.

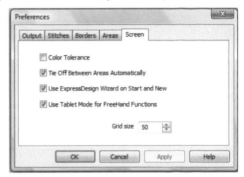
Suggested Image

4. From the top toolbar, begin a New file .

5. Select Create Express Embroidery, then Next.

6. View Picture 📷 and open the file: C:\4DEmbroidery\PictureLibrary\Clipart\ Designs\DESsquar\G0120352.WMF (*alternate image for this exercise is C:\4DEmbroidery\Samples\4DEmb\ Pics2\Celebration\1CCe003.png*)

Alternate Image

7. Choose Next. Rotation = 0°, Next.

8. On the Crop Picture screen, no changes are necessary, so choose Next again.

9. Design Size window: Select Fit Design to Hoop and change the hoop to Hoop Group = Pfaff 2170/2144/2140, Hoop Size = 225 mm x 140 mm Creative Large Hoop, Orientation = Horizontal. Choose OK, then Next.

10. The Reduce Colors window indicates three thread colors. Choose Next.

11. On the Choose Thread Colors window, change to the Madeira Rayon 40 thread range. Uncheck the Automatically Remove Background Color box. Leaving the box unchecked (open) converts the white area into an embroidery region so that it may be edited later. Choose Next to continue to the following screen.

12. In the Fabric and Stitch Style Options window, set the fabric type to Woven. Uncheck the Design Underlay box. Choose Next to begin generating the design.

13. Complete the new design by selecting Finish. The completed design should look like one of the following images:

To add underlay...or not to add underlay? That is the question. (OK, so maybe it's a question that only a digitizer would ask!) For most designs, it is best to check the design underlay box to add stabilizing stitches underneath the design. In this case, however, the white region will be converted into an open stipple fill area later. Placing a check mark in the Design Underlay box would produce visible underlay stitches in the final embroidery design. Therefore, in this exercise, we will not add underlay.

EDIT, CREATE, AND PICTURE TABS

Notice the three tabs at the lower left-hand corner of the screen. Choose design options in the

Create tab. Select and edit design regions in the Edit tab. Alter an image in the Picture tab.

The filmstrip at the left side of the Edit tab screen indicates the order in which the machine will stitch each region of the design. To select a region of the design to edit it, left click once on that region in the filmstrip or in the main design portion of the screen. The filmstrip moves to the selected region and selection handles encircle the area in the main screen.

SELECT WORK AREA

1. Select the Edit tab.

2. Using the filmstrip, scroll down to the upper left hand pink block. Left click once to select this region.

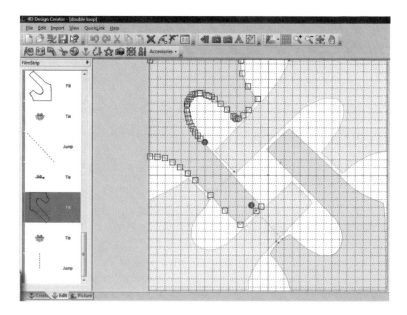

3. To edit this area, hover over the region and right click. Select Properties to open the Fill Properties screen.

(*For the alternate exercise, choose the red heart region*).

CHANGE FILL PROPERTIES

The Fill Properties screen has four tabs. The Patterns tab alters filled regions to one of over 250 fill patterns. The My Patterns tab shows patterns that you have created. The Density tab offers the capability to change the density of a region or to alter that region to gradient or multi-gradient fills. Change stitch angle, underlay, and compensation under the Options tab. Use the Conversion feature at the bottom of the Options tab to convert the selected region to another fill type (fill, motif fill, satin area, or specialty fill).

1. On the Patterns tab of the Fill Properties screen, change to fill pattern = 57 (Type the number "57" into the pattern box or choose Category = Arrows and then select the lower left hand square). Embossed should be unchecked.

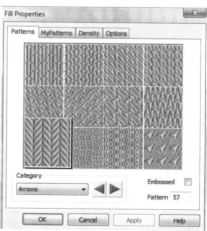

2. Under the Options tab, alter the angle to 225°. The other features remain unchanged, so select OK.

3. To view the changes made in this area, return to the Create tab. Notice the new fill pattern and fill angle.

4. To make more changes in the design, return to the Edit tab. Use the filmstrip area to select the lower right hand pink region (*alternate exercise –choose the inner white area*).

5. Right click on the area to open the Fill Properties screen. On the Fill tab, set the fill pattern to number 181. Choose the Options tab and ensure that the angle is still set to 225°. Choose OK. (For the alternate exercise, alter the inner white region to this fill pattern). Return to the Create tab at the lower left hand corner of the screen to view the changes.

CONVERT TO STIPPLE FILL

1. Under the Edit tab, select the white region of the design (look at the filmstrip to ensure that the correct area is selected). Right click to open the Fill Properties screen.

2. Choose the Options tab and set Conversion = Specialty Fill. Select OK to complete the conversion.

3. A second window opens entitled Specialty Fill Properties. Set Style = QuickStipple Fill. Note that the window changes and now Options is the only other tab available.

4. Choose the Options tab and select the following: Style = Curved, Spacing Gap = 3.0 mm, Stitch = Running and Stitch Length = 2.0mm. Complete the changes by clicking OK. [*Alternate image: Convert each of the four white regions outside the heart into stippling using the same process.*]

5. Return to the Create tab to view the new stippling.

A crisscross or "x" pattern in the background of an open specialty fill (such as stippling) indicates that the area includes underlay stitches. To avoid creating visible underlay in an open fill region, uncheck the Underlay box on the Change Thread Colors window of the Design Creator.

[In the alternate exercise, the example shown above includes the addition of a satin border around the heart.]

SAVE DESIGN

In 4D Design Creator, it is necessary to save a design at least twice—as a ".can" (design) file and as an embroidery file. (The preferred Pfaff embroidery format is ".vp3".) If the image has been edited, you must also save the picture file. (It is unnecessary to save the picture in this exercise.)

The regions of a ".can" file may be altered later, but it cannot be stitched out. The embroidery file (.vp3 or other machine format) will be stitched out. A simple way to remember the distinction is that a ".can" file *can* be edited. Always save the ".can" file first and then generate and save the embroidery file.

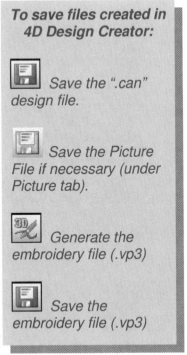

To save files created in 4D Design Creator:

Save the ".can" design file.

Save the Picture File if necessary (under Picture tab).

Generate the embroidery file (.vp3)

Save the embroidery file (.vp3)

SAVE .CAN FILE

1. With the Create tab active, choose File→Save As (or from the top toolbar).

2. In most cases, designs you have created will be saved in the My Designs folder. If this is not the active folder, use the down arrow and change to this folder.

3. The File Name defaults to the name of the original image. Since the original file name was not very descriptive, change the file name to "Double Loops". 4D Design Creator automatically adds the ".can" file extension so that the complete file name is now "Double Loops.can".

Alternate exercise file name: Class Heart

GENERATE STITCHES AND SAVE EMBROIDERY FILE

1. Choose 3D Create Stitches 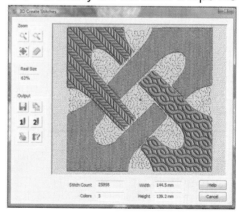 from the top toolbar. The window that opens provides a synopsis of the design information. If desired, print the design or send it directly to the embroidery machine from this window.

2. Before closing this window, save the design by choosing the Output File Save As icon ⬛. Save the file under the same name chosen for the .can file (in this case, "Double Loops".) The embroidery file will have a .vp3 file extension and will not overwrite the .can file saved earlier. It is important to give these files the same name so that you will know that the two files are associated with one another.

LOAD PICTURE

1. From the top toolbar, click Preferences and select the Screen tab. Ensure that the Color Tolerance box is deselected (unchecked).

2. Begin a new file.

3. Choose Load Picture for New Design, Next.

4. View Picture and open C:\4DEmbroidery\PictureLibrary \Clipart\Borders\BRDseasn\ G0429861.WMF. Select Next to proceed to the Rotate Picture window.

Alternate image is C:\4DEmbroidery\Samples\4DEmb\ Pics2\Holidays\ICHo006.png

5. It is not necessary to rotate or crop the picture, so choose Next twice to move to the remaining screen options.

6. On the Design Size window, select the Enter Design Size button, then set Enter Design Size = 80mm and turn on the Width button, Next.

7. Reduce the number of Thread colors to 3 and note that the right screen shows a preview of the reduced color image. The left screen shows the original image.

8. Choose Finish to complete the process.

1. From the Preferences icon located on the top toolbar , select the Areas tab and set the Fill Pattern = 10 and Angle = 50°. Underlay = Low, Satin Pattern = 0. Underlay ZigZag = checked and Edgewalk = unchecked. Select the Screen tab and uncheck the Color Tolerance button. Select the Stitches tab. Density Fill = 2, Satin = 3. Select the Borders tab and set Border Width = 1.5mm. Other options remain unchanged. OK to continue. Helpful Hint: remember that as density number decreases, the stitch density increases.

2. Ensure that the Create tab is active. From the top toolbar, select the arrow adjacent to Picture . Three choices are available: . Select Background On .

3. Click the small arrow adjacent to the Color Change icon . Select Pick Color and then click inside the red portion of the hat. 4D Design Creator suggests a red thread in your default thread range.

    Don't see all threads?

    Select the Show All Thread Ranges button.

    For the sake of clarity in this exercise, alter the color to Robison Anton Rayon 40, color number 2378 and then close the thread box with OK.

4. From the **left toolbar**, click the arrow next to Quickstitch Fill  and choose Quickstitch Fill . Tap inside the red hat area.

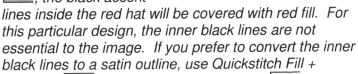

Using Quickstitch Fill 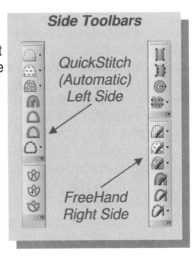*, the black accent lines inside the red hat will be covered with red fill. For this particular design, the inner black lines are not essential to the image. If you prefer to convert the inner black lines to a satin outline, use Quickstitch Fill + Autohole rather than Quickstitch Fill .*

5. Most of the icons in the program are grayed out indicating that they are not active. Right click to make them active and to stop adding fill.

Side Toolbars

QuickStitch (Automatic) Left Side

FreeHand Right Side

ADD RIPPLE PATTERN FILL TO HAT RIM

1. Insert a Color Change . Change the thread to Robison-Anton Rayon 40 color 2297.

2. Change to a new fill pattern. Select the Areas tab. Set Pattern = 233 and Angle = 80 degrees. Other options remain unchanged. Choose OK to close the Preferences window.

   An arrow adjacent to an icon indicates "more options." Click the arrow to view and select the additional options.

3. Using the arrow adjacent to the left toolbar Quickstitch

   Fill 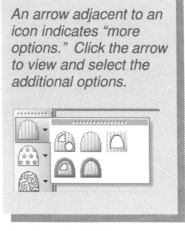, select

   Quickstitch Fill .

4. Click inside the white hat rim area.

5. Right click to deactivate the Quickstitch Fill function.

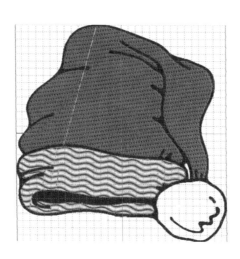

ADD MOTIF FILL TO HAT TASSEL

Since the tassel will be white, which is the last color used, it is not necessary to change the thread color this time.

1. Select the arrow adjacent to Quickstitch Motif Fill and choose Quickstitch Motif Fill [icon].

2. Click inside the white tassel. Right click to deactivate Quickstitch Motif Fill.

3. To alter this fill to a different pattern, choose the Edit tab.

4. Tap on the tassel region and then right click to open the Motif Fill Properties window.

5. For Motif 1, click the arrow next to Group and set it to Pfaff. Category = Decorative 1-A, Pattern = 11, Height and Width = 9.0mm. Proportional = checked. Change the Gap to Horizontal % = -6 (negative 6), Vertical % = -17. Change the Horizontal Offset to 45% and leave the Vertical Offset set to 0%. Notice how the motif shifts as these options are changed.

6. Close the Motif Fill Properties window with OK.

7. Return to the Create tab and view the new motif fill.

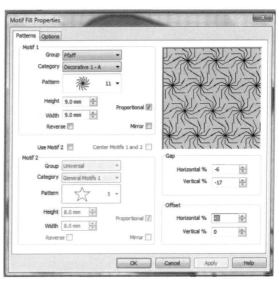

ADD BORDER

1. Choose the outline thread color by clicking the Color Change icon  and selecting Robison-Anton Rayon 40 color 2296. Close the thread selection box with OK.

2. Select Preferences . Under the Areas tab, set Fill Pattern = 1.

3. Choose the arrow adjacent to Quick Stitch Fill  and select Quick Stitch Fill + Auto Hole + Border .

   Alternate exercise: Use Quadruple Trace  rather than Quick Stitch Fill + Auto Hole + Border.

4. Tap on the black border area.

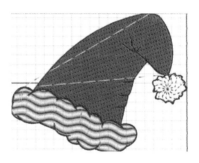

Suggested Exercise   *Alternate Exercise*

SAVE .CAN AND .VP3 FILES

1. Save the .can (design) file as Santa Hat.can by choosing File Save As ![disk icon] from the top toolbar. Again, ensure that the file is saved in the My Designs folder and that the file name matches the corresponding embroidery design.
2. Generate the embroidery design with 3D Generate Stitches ![icon]. Save ![disk icon] the .vp3 embroidery design in the My Designs folder. Two files should exist: Santa Hat.vp3 and Santa Hat.can.

ADDITIONAL FEATURES

Stitch Order: When preparing a custom design, create stitch areas in a logical order so that jump stitches will be easier to trim (e.g. from top to bottom, left to right or clockwise). Remember that the embroidery machine stitches the design in the order it was digitized. To change the order of stitching in 4D Design Creator, activate the Edit tab. Select a region of the design in the filmstrip. Left click, hold, and drag the selected item to the new location. Be cautious in using this feature to ensure that the new stitch order will still produce an attractive design.

3-Dimensional Design: Try changing the patterns and pattern angles in a design to achieve different effects. Think about a painter painting in different directions. Unique stitch angles and patterns provide a 3-dimensional look for your custom designs.

Filter Objects: In the filmstrip of the Edit tab, use one of the Filter Objects options to hide all of a given stitch type (such as all jump stitches or all tie-offs, etc).

Quick versus Freehand: In the Create tab, notice that the icons on the left are similar to the icons at the right side of the screen. Icons on the left side are Quick (or automatic). For example, QuickStitch Fill ⛰automatically places a fill pattern in the selected area. At the right side of the screen are Freehand features. For example, use Freehand Fill ◣ to draw in a fill region manually.

Outlines: An outline around a design is usually the last area stitched so that it is on top of all the other stitching. Since it needs to be the last area stitched, it should be the last area digitized. There are several choices for outlining. Quadruple Trace ⟨⟩ outlines with a running stitch tracing the line with four layers of stitching. Trace options include double, quadruple or constant width stitches. Create satin outlines easily using a Quick border such as QuickStitch Fill plus Border ⛰ or QuickStitch Fill + AutoHole + Border ⛰. Similar options place an automatic border around motif or specialty fill regions.

QuickStitch Border ⛰ prepares a satin border without any fill regions. Sometimes it is easier to select the outlines in a picture when the design is viewed in two dimensions rather than three. Toggle between the 2-dimensional view and the 3-dimensional view by clicking the 3D icon from the top toolbar. Another method for adding an outline is to prepare two designs—one with the design (no border), and one with only the border. Then superimpose the border design over the non-border design. (Remember to lay down the non-border design first and the border second so that the border is stitched out last).

Image Editing: The Picture tab features simple photo or image editing tools. Explore how the embroidery design changes if the image is converted to black and white or sepia. If the original picture is edited, save the picture file, the .can file, and the .vp3 file.

Other Features to Explore: Feathering   adds blending to the edge of a region.

Specialty Fills: Many specialty fills are available including Radial, Contour, Shape, Stipple, and Spiral (normal, gradient, or multi-gradient). To convert an area to a specialty fill, activate the Edit tab. Right click on the region. Select the Options tab and use Conversion to change the region to a Specialty Fill. Exercise 1 of this chapter demonstrated stipple fill. The examples below illustrate some of the other specialty fills.

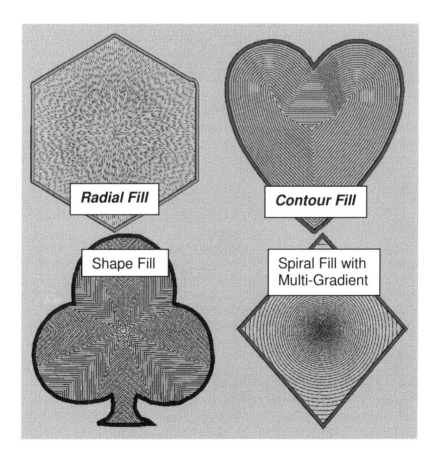

Radial Fill

Contour Fill

Shape Fill

Spiral Fill with Multi-Gradient

INTRODUCTION

Beautiful cross-stitch designs from an embroidery machine?
Absolutely! With 4D Cross Stitcher, you can create custom
machine embroidered cross-stitch designs. Rather than
spending hours working by hand, let the machine do the work!
4D Cross Stitcher converts a digital photo or graphic image into
a cross-stitched design or gives many options to create a design
"from scratch." Choose the number of thread colors, hoop size,
and cross stitch size. Prepare cross-stitched lettering with
built-in fonts or create a new font from any True Type font on
your computer. Add cross-stitch backgrounds. In this exercise,
you will learn how to convert a clip-art image into a cross-stitch
design, insert a border, and then add cross-stitch lettering to
complete the design.

CREATE QUICKCROSS DESIGN

1. Launch 4D Embroidery Extra (Start → All Programs → 4D Embroidery System then 4D Embroidery Extra).

   From the top toolbar, select 4D Cross Stitch .

2. When the Cross Stitch Design Wizard opens, choose Create QuickCross Design, then Next.

3. Load Picture. Open the file C:/4DEmbroidery/PictureLibrary/ ClipArt/Borders/BRDmisc/G0205720.vp3. Select Open and then Next.

> *Alternate image is C:\4DEmbroidery\ Samples\4DEmb\Pics2\Fashion\ 1CFa21.png*

4. On the Grid and Hoop window, Grid Control: Fine Movement = unchecked, Show Grid = checked, Rectangular Selection = checked. Hoop Size: Cross Stitch Size = 1.4mm, Proportional = checked. Click Select Hoop: Hoop Group = Pfaff 2170/2144/2140, Hoop Size = 225mm x 140mm Creative Large Hoop, Orientation = Vertical. Close the hoop selection window by clicking OK.

5. Reduce the Width to 98 Crosses.

   A QuickCross design automatically fills the selected hoop size. Since precise alignment is critical for an attractive embroidered cross-stitch, it is helpful to reduce the size of the design slightly. Although this is not essential, it is a practical step to make the design easier to stitch. In this exercise, reducing the width to 98 crosses also reduces the design size to approximately

137 mm x 172 mm—effectively allowing 3 mm of movement within the hoop to align the design when it is stitched out. (Alternate image is approx. 137mm x 148mm.)

6. Proceed to the next window by choosing Next.

7. On the Cross Stitch Design Wizard: Start with Colors window, set the Thread Range = Robison Anton Rayon 40 and Number of Colors = 12. *(Alternate image: 8 colors).*

   The default maximum setting for the number of thread colors is twelve (there may be fewer than twelve). To increase or decrease the number of thread changes, adjust the number of colors in this step.

8. Choose Next to proceed.

9. Check the Merge Identical Thread Colors box. On the Thread Colors window, the remaining default options are acceptable. If needed, add or delete thread colors in this step. The left window shows the selected image and the right window previews the color of the cross-stitch design using the thread colors chosen. The cross-stitch image changes based upon the colors of thread chosen.

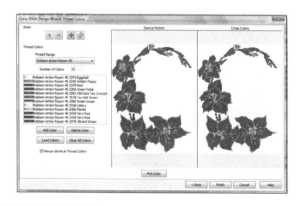

---

10. Complete the Design Wizard by selecting Finish.

REMOVE BACKGROUND CROSSES

A Quick Cross design converts an entire image into crosses. In hand cross-stitch, however, often crosses do not fill the entire design area. To make this design appear more like a hand-stitched cross-stitch, we will remove unnecessary background crosses. Removing the additional background stitches also reduces the time needed to embroider the design. Cross-stitched designs are time consuming to embroider, so it is wise to consider this when designing a new cross-stitch. A larger cross-stitch size corresponds to a larger "X." In general, the size of the "X" determines the resolution of the final cross-stitched image. The more X's, the higher the resolution of the image, but the more time it will take to stitch and to clip threads. Experiment with several different sizes to find the one that best suits your project.

1. On the Design tab, select the Color Configuration icon from the right hand side of the screen.

2. The Color Configuration window appears. Ensure that the Order tab is active and click to select the first color, Robison Anton Rayon 40 2343 Eggshell. Select Remove Color. Answer Yes when the program asks if

you really want to delete this entire color. Close the Color Configuration window by selecting OK.

Use this feature with caution because all stitches of the first color will be removed, regardless of where they are located in the design. In this case, all of the background is eggshell and none of the floral image uses this color. Therefore, it is acceptable to delete the color altogether.

3. From the far left side of the screen, choose Flood Fill ✎. Select the Eraser ✐ as the "color" of the flood fill. Click inside the celery colored center oval area to remove these stitches. Flood Fill ✎ only paints (or in this case, erases) contiguous (adjacent) stitches. To erase other stitches, continue Flood Filling these areas with the Erase color. Zoom in $^{Q+}$ to view individual stitches if necessary. (*Alternate exercise: skip this step since step 2 removed the center stitches for this image.*)

ADD TRUETYPE FONT

There are two types of cross-stitch fonts, True Type Text and Fixed Text.

4D Cross Stitcher includes many Fixed Text fonts that are pre-installed in the software. Many look similar to hand cross-stitch lettering. The size of these fonts is fixed and, therefore, cannot be altered. To preview the Fixed Fonts, select the button entitled Fixed Font (the top of the right hand window) and select View Font ▣. Scroll through the available fonts. The name of the font also indicates the size (i.e. Old Eng Cross 15 = Old English font, the height of a capital "A" is 15 crosses).

A second type of font is a TrueType Text font. Choices include TrueType fonts installed on your computer from a word processing program or similar programs. Some fonts on your computer may not be TrueType fonts, and therefore, may not appear in the list of available choices. To create a new font, select the TrueType Text button from the top right hand side of the screen. Click the arrow adjacent to the font name box. Scroll through the listing to choose one. Some fonts will produce more pleasing cross-stitched letters than others, so experiment with different choices to find an attractive font for your project.

1. Activate the Letter tab (lower right corner of screen).

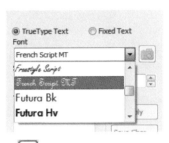

2. The demonstration font is "French Script MT." Choose a similar font if this one is unavailable on your computer.

3. Deselect the Bold [B] and Italic [I] buttons. Alignment is Centered [≡] and Height = 18.

4. Type the desired wording into the text box. Hold down the Shift key and hit the Enter key to add multiple lines of text. Demonstration: "Cyndy" [hold Shift key and hit Enter key] "&" [hold Shift, hit Enter] "Sam" [Shift, Enter] "7-7-07" (do not type the quotation marks).

5. The size of the text box in millimeters, and the width and height of crosses, appears just underneath the text box.

6. Select Place TrueType Text As: Crosses/Fill Pattern and check the Smooth box.

7. Left click the colored Cross box and select Robison Anton Rayon 40 color 2378. Since this font does not have an outline, it is unnecessary to alter the outline color.

8. Select Apply and then move the text box to center it inside the floral border.

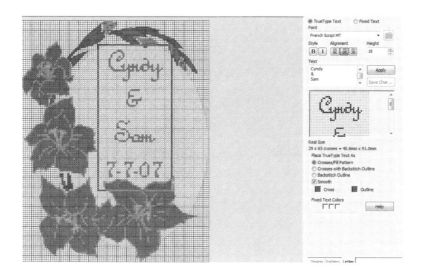

Alternate exercise: Follow the same steps as in the suggested exercise, but choose Futura Lt font, height=10, Text="Cyndy" [Shift + Enter] "& Sam" [Shift + Enter] "7-7-07", color = RA 40 wt 2296.

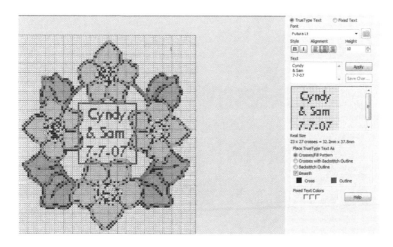

GENERATE STITCHES AND SAVE FILES

1. Return to the Design tab and save ![icon] the editable cross-stitch design as C:/4D Embroidery/MyDesigns/floral frame.krz.

2. All cross-stitch designs must be saved as an embroidery file also. To create the embroidery design, choose 3D Generate Stitches ![icon] from the top toolbar. Note the size and the number of stitches in the design. Save ![icon] the design as C:/4D Embroidery/My Designs/floral frame.vp3.

3. Close 4D Cross Stitcher.

To Save Cross Stitch Designs

![icon] Save .krz file

![icon] 3D Generate Stitches

![icon] Save the .vp3 embroidery file

Create backgrounds or shapes from many cross-stitch patterns in the Pattern tab. The toolbar on the left side of the screen shows various types of cross-stitches that may be added, such as simple cross, backstitch, minicross, etc. Click a thread color from the right toolbar area and then select one of the stitch icons from the left side of the screen. Click or click-and-drag the mouse inside the design to add one or multiple cross-stitches. Right click to deselect these options. To add a new thread color, select Add Color 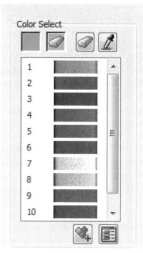.

Add cross-stitch shapes or a background using tools located on the Pattern tab. To add a filled background, check Use Fill Pattern and then select the pattern you would like to use. Change background thread colors by clicking on the color.

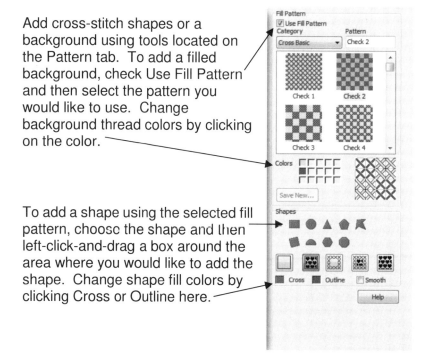

To add a shape using the selected fill pattern, choose the shape and then left-click-and-drag a box around the area where you would like to add the shape. Change shape fill colors by clicking Cross or Outline here.

4D STITCH EDITOR

INTRODUCTION

With 4D Stitch Editor, you can morph a design, or a portion of the design, with ripple, twirl, or other unusual effects. You can alter filled regions to new fill patterns, add border shapes and background appliqués, edit a design using many advanced features, or split a design along a user-defined line.

EXERCISE 1: "STAR QUILT BLOCK"

EXPRESS CREATE A QUILT BLOCK DESIGN

1. Link to 4D Embroidery Extra. It should be an open tab on the lower left hand corner of your screen.

2. Select Hoop ⬚. Check the box to Enter Hoop Size and set the Hoop Size = 100mm x 100mm, OK. (This constrains the design to a size of 100mm x 100mm. It does not necessarily mean that you will stitch the design in a hoop of that size.)

3. Begin the Express Design Creator ▨. Select Create Express Embroidery, then Next.

4. View Picture 📷 and open the folder C:\4DEmbroidery\PictureLibrary\ Clipart\Backgrounds\BAKpattn. Scroll down and open the file G0132660.WMF.

Alternate image:
C:\4DEmbroidery\Samples\4DEmb
Pics2\Geometrics\1CGe17.png

---

5. Choose Next to continue to the Rotate Picture window and then Next again to move to the Crop Picture window. *Alternate image: Rotate image 45°.*

6. Hold the Ctrl key, left-click and drag the blue square located at the bottom right hand corner of the selection box. Release the mouse to crop the image to a single square as shown in the picture below. Next to continue. *Do not crop the alternate image.*

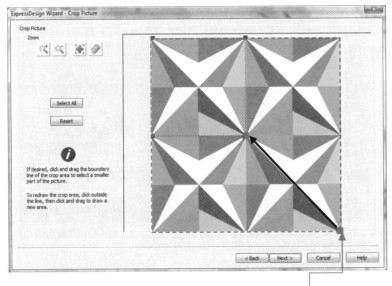

Left-click, hold, and drag square to crop picture

7. Reduce to 7 colors and continue with Next.

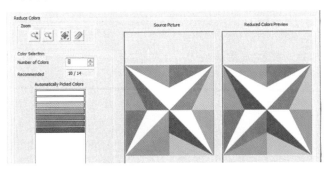

8. Set the thread range to Sulky Rayon 40. Double click on each color and change to the following colors:
   1. 1061 Pale Yellow
   2. 1819 Outback
   3. 1077 Jade Tint
   4. 1181 Rust
   5. 1311 Mulberry
   6. 1203 Lt. Weathered Blue
   7. 1298 Dk. Plum

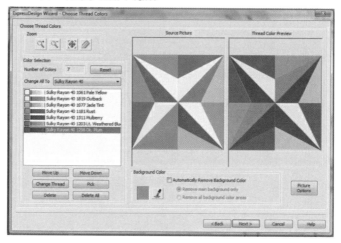

9. Proceed to the final screen. Set the Fabric type to Woven and uncheck the Underlay box. Next and then Finish.

10. Save the file 💾 as Star Quilt Block.vp3.

OPEN DESIGN IN 4D STITCH EDITOR

1. From 4D Embroidery Extra, launch 4D Stitch Editor .

2. Select Hoop 🔲. Hoop Group = Pfaff
    2170/2144/2140, 225mm x 140mm Creative Large
    Hoop, Orientation = Horizontal, OK.

3. Open Star Quilt Block by selecting View 📷. Browse
    ⋯ to open c:/4D Embroidery/My Designs/Star Quilt
    Block.vp3.

REMOVE STITCH POINTS

1. Notice the three tabs at the lower right hand corner of the
    screen. Ensure that the Design tab is active.

2. Select Draw Next Color Block ≫ so
    that the first color block is shown (Sulky
    Rayon 40 1061 Pale Yellow). Only the
    stitches in this color block should be
    visible. The area shown will be the area
    modified in the successive steps.

    An alternate method of selecting the
    first color block is to deselect each of the remaining color
    blocks. To toggle between hiding and viewing a color
    block, left click the box adjacent to the thread color.

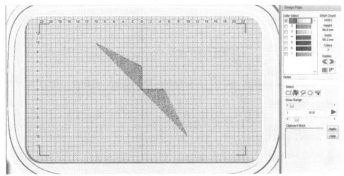

3. Select the Pattern Make tab.

4. Choose Remove Stitch Points
   . This converts the active region to a simple satin fill area.

In most cases, it is best to remove the stitch points in an existing pattern before applying a stamp fill to the area. If you do not remove the stitch points, the stamp will be applied over the existing pattern.

ADD STAMP FILL

1. Select the arrow next to the Stamps box and choose the Miscellaneous 4 stamp pattern set. Choose the shape shown.
2. Select the stamp size: Small Stamp [◇].
3. Ensure that Angle is set to 0°.
4. Stamp fill the entire area [▩].

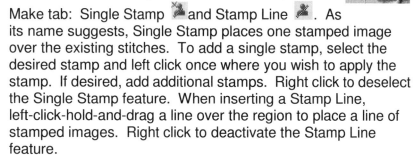

Notice two other stamp fill choices on the Pattern Make tab: Single Stamp [▦] and Stamp Line [▦]. As its name suggests, Single Stamp places one stamped image over the existing stitches. To add a single stamp, select the desired stamp and left click once where you wish to apply the stamp. If desired, add additional stamps. Right click to deselect the Single Stamp feature. When inserting a Stamp Line, left-click-hold-and-drag a line over the region to place a line of stamped images. Right click to deactivate the Stamp Line feature.

Both small and large stamps may be used. A small stamp is approximately 6.4mm on the longest size and a large stamp is about three times the size of the same small stamp.

Only the region that is visible on the Pattern Make tab will be stamped. Thus, if the entire design is visible, the entire design will be stamped, and if a portion of the design is visible, then only the visible region will be stamped.

ADD SECOND STAMP FILL

1. Modify the angle to 180° and Stamp Fill  a second time. *Do not remove the stitch points this time since the second fill will be added over the first.*
2. Return to the Design tab. To view the entire embroidery design, Draw All Stitches 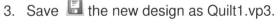.
3. Save 💾 the new design as Quilt1.vp3.

ADD BORDER

Alternate image: skip this section. The alternate design has a border already.

1. Click the Preferences icon 🖽 , Border tab. Set Width = 3.0, Density = 4, Underlay = checked. Change the border color to Sulky Rayon 40 color = 505. OK.

2. Select the Modify tab. In the Border/Appliqué box, choose Draw Border Shape 🔲 and select shape number 1 (square).

3. Hold the Ctrl key while you left-click-hold-and-drag a square around the edge of the quilt block.

4. Select the arrow adjacent to the Create Border icon 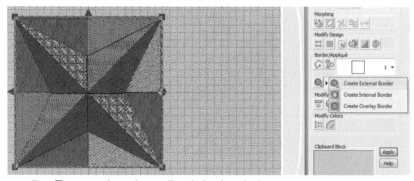 and choose Create External Border . This adds a dark blue border around the quilt block and removes stitches outside of this border.

5. Ensure that the edited design is in the foreground. Save 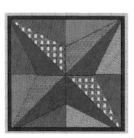 the edited design in the My Designs folder as quilt2.vp3.

Notice the two tabs located at the bottom left hand corner of the screen. The first tab is Quilt1.vp3. Selecting  the first tab brings the original design to the foreground. The second tab is the edited design (Quilt2.vp3).

Two other border types are available: Create Internal Border (creates a border and removes stitches inside the border) and Create Overlay Border (places a border over the object, but does not remove any stitches).

An entire design or a discrete position in a design may be "morphed" (altered). Global morphing 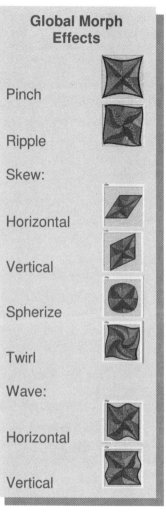 alters an entire design (or the visible area) with one of eight morphing effects including pinch, ripple, skew horizontal, skew vertical, spherize, twirl, wave horizontal and wave vertical.

The Global Morphing Effects window previews both the original design and the altered design. The drop down arrow next to Pinch opens a box to select the desired morphing function. One or more slider bars modify the intensity of the effect.

1. From the Modify tab, choose Global Morph 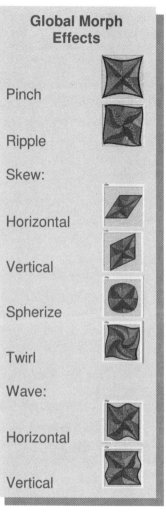.
2. Select Pinch and move the slider bar to Intensity = 8 to visualize how this feature alters the design. The right hand window is only a preview of the morphing effect, so no changes are permanent until you finalize the morph with OK.
3. Finalize the Pinch morphed design with OK and then return to the Design tab.

Global Morph Effects

Pinch

Ripple

Skew:

Horizontal

Vertical

Spherize

Twirl

Wave:

Horizontal

Vertical

Feel free to explore other global morph options to view how these effects alter the design.

POINT MORPHING

Point morphing effects include magnet 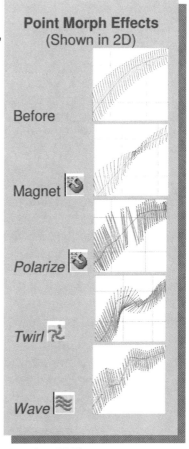, polarize , twirl , and wave . These four effects only modify a single point in the design. For example, to wave a small region, left click the area to place a single wave at that point. Right click to deselect the morph feature. You can always

Undo a morph if you did not like the change.

1. Return to the Design tab and turn on Ghost Mode . This visualization mode shows one color block at a time with the remaining color blocks "ghosted" out (shown in white).

2. Use Draw Next Color Block to step through the color blocks to the eighth block (Sulky Rayon 40 color 505).

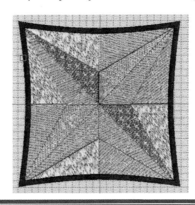

3. Move to the Modify tab and select Wave Morphing 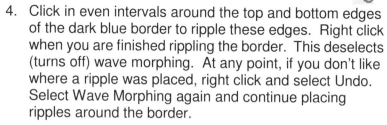.

4. Click in even intervals around the top and bottom edges of the dark blue border to ripple these edges. Right click when you are finished rippling the border. This deselects (turns off) wave morphing. At any point, if you don't like where a ripple was placed, right click and select Undo. Select Wave Morphing again and continue placing ripples around the border.

5. Draw All Stitches ▥ to return to viewing the design without ghosted stitches.

6. Optimize ⊕ the design to remove any unnecessary short stitches automatically.

7. Save the design 💾 as quilt3.vp3.

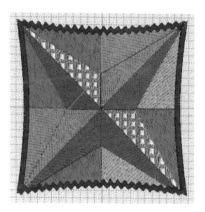
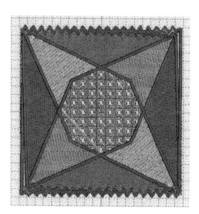

ADDITIONAL FEATURES

Stitch Player: On the Design tab, use Draw Range to select a portion of the design. Select Stitch Player ▶ to preview the stitch sequence. Fast Forward ▶▶ or Rewind ◀◀ (among other functions) to move to specific regions of the design.

Resize/Rotate: On the Modify tab, resize or rotate a design or portion of the design.

Compensate Stitches: ⇔ makes the active embroidery area bolder (does not alter the number of stitches, just lengthens the stitches). Modify tab.

Density Advisor: ▨ shows the regions of a design that are too dense and offers the capability to reduce the density of these areas. Modify tab.

Appliqué Borders: Three options are available to create appliqué borders ▣▶: Create External Appliqué ⬤, Create Internal Appliqué ⬤ and Create Overlay Appliqué ⬤.

Design Separator ▦ splits a design along a moveable line. It is useful when a design is larger than can be stitched inside a particular hoop, or when only a portion of a design is needed.

Special Stitch Commands: Stitches may be modified by Inserting a Color Change ⊕, Inserting a Stop Command ⊗ (stops the machine so that you can trim threads or trim an appliqué), Inserting a Trim Command ✄ (the machine auto-trims threads), Deleting Commands ⊠ (remove existing trims, stops, etc), Inserting Stitches ⌶, or Inserting one of nine types of Tie-offs ✥▶.

4D SKETCH

INTRODUCTION

With 4D Sketch, you can add thread painting with or without printable fabric in the background, add stippling inside the embroidery hoop, insert stitch-regulated or speed-sensitive stitching, and add calligraphy, rotational zigzag, or standard zigzag stitches. The Wacom Volito 2 pen tablet integrates seamlessly with 4D Sketch and also works with all 4D software modules as well as other software programs on your computer. It is available as a separate purchase. In this section, you will learn how to use 4D Sketch, how to install and use the Volito 2 pen tablet, and how to use an associated drawing program, ArtRage. (The ArtRage program is included with the purchase of the pen tablet.)

INSTALL PEN TABLET AND ARTRAGE

Plug the Tablet into a USB port on your computer. Place the Wacom Volito 2 installation disk into the CD Disk drive on the computer and follow the installation procedures. Continue by installing the ArtRage program, which is also on the same disk. Follow the procedures on the disk to register the pen tablet via internet (or register via mail if internet access is not available). The registration process will ask which tablet model to register. Register the Volito 2 pen tablet.

It is essential to understand how using a pen tablet differs from using a mouse. Although all 4D Sketch features work with a mouse or laptop touchpad, many people find that using the pen tablet is easier and more precise. Expect that the pen tablet will have a short learning curve for those who are accustomed to using a mouse or the touchpad on a laptop computer. A mouse or touchpad uses a "pick up and slide" action. The pen tablet is designed such that the rectangular work surface on the tablet corresponds with the rectangular shape of the computer screen. As you move to the top left of the tablet, the screen cursor also moves to the top left of the computer screen. The action of left-click, left-click-and-drag, or right click on a mouse is also different on the pen tablet.

• Plan to work through the Pen Tablet tutorial to learn more about the action of the pen. To start the tutorial, go to Start→All Programs→Tablet→Tutorial. This tutorial takes about 15 minutes and orients you to the use of the tablet.

• The Wacom pen tablet is speed and pressure sensitive for programs that utilize these features. 4D Sketch is speed sensitive, but not pressure sensitive. The ArtRage program is both speed and pressure sensitive.

• The pen tablet can replace a mouse for any program on the computer (such as word processing or photo editing software). The precision offered by the tablet is particularly helpful with graphic software such as photo editing.

• Some people with wrist or hand problems find that using a pen tablet is more comfortable than using a mouse.

- The pen tip registers location when it is approximately 3-5mm above the surface of the tablet. Hover over an area on the screen to see the screen cursor. Do not place the pen directly onto the tablet at this point, as this is another action associated with the tablet. Practice moving the pen around the tablet to become accustomed to hovering over the pen surface.

- Tapping on the tablet once is the same as a left-click on a mouse (or laptop touchpad).

- There are two buttons on the pen. The button closest to the pen tip (bottom button) is equivalent to a mouse right-click. The top button is equivalent to a left double-click on a mouse. You can re-configure the action associated with each of these buttons by opening the tablet properties (Start→All Programs→Tablet→Tablet Properties).

- To place a selection box around an area of the screen, hold the tip of the pen on the tablet surface, drag a box around the area, and then lift the pen tip.

- Tapping the tablet surface twice quickly is equivalent to a mouse double click.

- If you prefer to change the action that is associated with each of the buttons, change the tablet properties by selecting "Tablet Properties" from your computer desktop.

- Start the ArtRage program by selecting Start→All Programs→ArtRage Wacom Edition→ArtRage Wacom Edition.

- Seven art tools are available including a paintbrush, a crayon, a pencil, chalks, felt pens, a palette knife and an eraser.

- Load "Tracing Paper" to place a background image on the screen. Select the half-circle at the bottom of the screen to choose the preferred background image.

- Selecting "File→New Painting" brings up options to change the dimensions of the artwork and the type of canvas. "Tracing Paper" can also be loaded here.

- Artwork is saved in a *.ptg format. Since this is not a common image format, select File→Export As Image to save the artwork in a more common format such as *.bmp, *.jpg or *.png. Use one of these three formats to bring artwork into 4D Sketch as a background image for thread painting.

- To start a new art design, select a tool (pencil, paintbrush, etc), then select the preferred color. The slider bar at the far right selects the color range and the quarter-circle area alters the shading of that color. Select the width of a tool by adjusting the + or − buttons in the circle of tool width (lower left-hand side of the screen). Some tools have other special features such as drawing with the tip or the side of a pencil.

- The palette knife only spreads existing paint that is already on the canvas.

- The palette knife and the paintbrush remain "dirty" after choosing a new color. Dip them in the water cup to clean them off or select "Auto Clean" to clean them each time you choose a new paint color.

- Since the tablet is pressure sensitive, pressing down harder on the tablet will place more paint, chalk, etc on the canvas and change the width and other features of a drawing tool.

- A paintbrush will run out of paint. Lift the pen from the tablet and start again. This is like dipping the brush in more paint.

PRINTABLE FABRICS

Although 4D Sketch does not require the use of printable fabric underneath an embroidery project, using these specialty fabrics allows you to create traditional thread painting with the simplicity of drawing stitches on a mouse or pen tablet. Exercise 1 demonstrates how to design this type of thread painting.

There are several manufacturers of printable fabrics, and consequently, there is some variation in the preparation depending on the brand purchased. In general, though, these fabrics come in 8 ½" x 11" sheets and on rolls similar to banner paper. They are designed to be printed on a home inkjet printer. An adhesive paper backing is fused onto fabric, allowing the fabric to be printed. Fabric types include silk, cotton, canvas and others. After printing the image on the fabric, peel away the paper backing and wash (or wet) the fabric to set the ink dyes. Follow the instructions in the package, since the process varies between manufacturers and fabric types. Inkjet printable fabrics are not designed for use in a laser printer.

4D Sketch inserts alignment stitches as the first color in the design. To avoid extra holes in the fabric, advance one stitch at a time through the alignment stitches without stitching them (lower the needle via the hand wheel to align each stitch without actually stitching it).

DESIGN WIZARD OPTIONS

When you start 4D Sketch, or if you begin a new design, the Design Wizard opens with the following options:

Load Picture for New Embroidery – Loads a background picture to begin thread painting over the picture or to use the picture as a traceable background image.

Load Picture and Embroidery – Loads both a background picture and an embroidery design.

Load Embroidery – Loads only an embroidery design.

Start a New Embroidery with no Picture – Draw stitches free-hand.

ALIGNMENT OPTIONS

If you plan to use printable fabric underneath an embroidery design to create a thread painting, it is important to align the embroidery properly over the fabric. Alignment options include:

Place Crosses on Picture: Select at least two locations on the background picture and place a "+" shaped alignment stitch over that point. The Pfaff Creative Vision and the Pfaff 2170 have precise rotational positioning that works extremely well with this feature. Rotational Alignment on the Creative Vision is precise to .01°. The 2170 series rotates a design in 0.5° increments. The 2124 and 2134 machines are limited to 1° rotation changes.

Automatic Corners: Automatically place an alignment stitch at each corner of the design.

None: If the design already has alignment stitches, or you prefer not to use them, select this option.

4D SKETCH EXERCISE 1: "3D FLOWER"

LOAD FLOWER PICTURE

1. Start 4D Sketch  by launching it from 4D Extra. The "Load Design Wizard" pop-up window opens. Select Load Picture for New Embroidery.

2. Change Hoop ⬜ to Hoop Group = Pfaff 2170/2144/2140, Hoop = 225mm x 140mm, Vertical Orientation, (*Alternate image – Horizontal Orientation*) then OK and Next.

3. View Picture 📷 and scroll down to open the file C:\4DEmbroidery\PictureLibrary\ Photos\Plants\PLAflora\p0303561.jpg. Select Next three times.

> *Alternate image: C:\4DEmbroidery\ Samples\Sketch\Pics3\PhotoFlowers\ OrangeFlower.jpg*

4. Set the Picture Height = 190mm. [*Alternate image: Height =130mm*]

> *Reduce Picture Height slightly to leave room to align the design precisely over the printable fabric.*

5. For the first thread color, select Pick Color 🖊 and then click inside a dark pink section of the flower petal. 4D Sketch finds the closest thread color to the selected area. For this exercise, use Robison Anton 40 wt rayon color 2508. [*Alternate image, color 2397*]

6. Choose Next and then Automatic Corners.

7. Select Finish.

1. Fade the Background Picture ▨. [*To toggle through the three background picture choices, successively click on the picture icons* ▨ *(background on),* ▨ *(background off), and* ▨ *(fade background).*]

2. Zoom In ▨ to the flower area to begin free-motion thread painting.

3. Choose Free Motion ▨. Draw around the outline of the flower. If you are using a mouse, hold the left button while you draw. Release it when you finish the line.

4. Right click to deselect Free Motion when you are finished adding the outline.

The faster you draw, the farther apart the stitches become. The slower you draw, the closer the stitches are. Being "zoomed in" affects the stitch length. Use the Free Motion Stitch Speed slider to adjust the ration between drawing speed and stitch length.

Explore another form of free-hand stitching by selecting the Quilt Motion icon 7. Hold down the Shift key to hide the jump stitches. Trace around a few more flower petals. Notice that Quilt Motion evenly spaces all stitches. The stitch length is determined not by the speed of drawing, but by the Free Motion Stitch Speed slider bar. When you are finished, right click to deselect the Quilt Motion tool.

> *Hide jump stitches by holding the Shift key*

A few helpful suggestions for drawing stitches using 4D Sketch:

*   Lift your hand off the pen tablet occasionally (or release the mouse) when you draw. Then continue drawing where you stopped. Use Undo 🔙 and Redo 🔜 to return to the last point where you lifted your hand off the tablet in case you make a mistake.

*   Try to avoid jump stitches. The machine stitches the design in the order that the stitches are drawn. To minimize jump stitches, start drawing from one side of the picture and work around the design in a logical order. When necessary, retrace existing lines to continue to the next line of stitching. This also reduces embroidery time by reducing the time needed to stop and clip additional threads.

1. Zoom To Fit  to see the entire design.

2. Insert a Color Change to Robison Anton Rayon 40 color 2466.

3. The "X" indicates the location of the last stitch. It also shows where the new stitches will begin.

Adjust the Free Motion Stitch Speed slider bar to change the density of the satin stitch in relation to drawing speed.

Free Motion Stitch Speed

Slow (100) — Fast (1000)

Zigzag ←   →Satin

4. Use Rotational Zigzag to trace a flower stamen. Remember to hold down the shift key to hide the jump stitch. Set the Zigzag width to 5.0mm. Taper the next flower stamen using the "Z" key on the computer keyboard. ("X" widens the zigzag stitch and "Z" tapers the zigzag). Trace each of the outer stamens of the flower. Right click to deselect Rotational Zigzag.

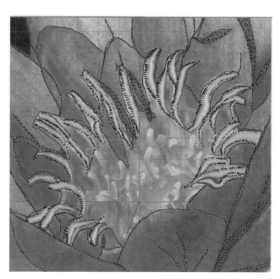

1. Move to the Motif tab at the lower right hand corner of the screen. Select Motif Group = Universal, Category = General Motifs 1, Pattern = 3 . Minimum Gap = 0.0mm, Fit to Line = checked, Final Motif = Complete. Size: Height = 6.0mm, Width =9.0mm. Proportional = checked. Stitch = Running.

2. Select Draw Motifs, Motif Motion ⟋. Begin drawing a motif line in a loose serpentine motion around the center of the flower. Right click to deselect Motif Motion when you are finished.

3. Save the Design As 🖫 "Pink Flower". Then select File→Save Picture to save the background picture as "Pink Flower 190 mm" (a reminder of the picture size).

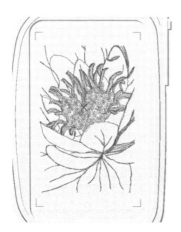

Embroidery Only

Embroidery with Printable Fabric image in background

Example of Alternate image thread painting design.

ADDITIONAL FEATURES

 Single Stitch – Add one stitch at a time.

 Free Motion – Draw speed sensitive stitching.

 Horizontal ZigZag – Draw satin or zigzag stitches at an angle (adjust by changing the calligraphy angle). Speed sensitive. The width is set by adjusting "ZigZag Width" or by using the "X" key on the keyboard to increase zigzag width and the "Z" key to decrease zigzag width.

 Rotational ZigZag – Draw satin or zigzag stitches perpendicular to the pen direction (follows the same conventions as the horizontal pen width).

Calligraphy – Add calligraphy. The angle of satin stitches is adjustable. The density is speed sensitive.

Quilt Motion – Stitch regulated drawing tool. Adjust the quilt motion stitch length in Preferences ▦ under the Stitches tab.

Insert Stitch - Toggles between options to add stitches at the selected stitch point or to add them at the end of the embroidery.

Editing selection tools – Make Block from Visible Area, Polygon Select, Freehand Select, and Box Select.

Erase Stitches – Erases stitches.

Stitch Player – "Play" the stitches in the order that they will be stitched. Use fast forward, rewind, etc., to move through the stitches.

Draw All Stitches – Display all stitches in the design.

Preferences – Set options such as quilt motion stitch length, maximum and minimum zigzag stitch width, and screen grid size.

- Use the Quilt Motion tool to add stippling inside the embroidery hoop. Raise the pen off the surface of the touch pad occasionally and use Undo to go back to the last time the pen was lifted if the stippling is not satisfactory.

- Coordinate 4D Sketch with other 4D Embroidery modules and add stitches easily. Copy a design to the clipboard in one 4D Embroidery software module, then Paste it into 4D Sketch. Add stitches, then Copy the changes from 4D Sketch, return to the first module, and Paste the changes. This can be a great way to create underlay stitches for a custom appliqué or to add an individual touch to a project such as calligraphy or even your own embroidered signature.

- Rather than loading a picture as the background, scan in a picture of a garment (in 4D Sketch Wizard). Draw in placement stitches over a location such as a neckline or seam line. Stitch the placement threads with dissolvable thread. Precisely align the garment over seam lines and then wash away the dissolvable thread when the project is complete—PERFECT alignment on important projects such as heirloom sewing.

- Make custom quilt labels by using Quilt Motion or Free Motion to write your own signature in stitches.

INTRODUCTION

4D Picture Stitch converts a digital photo or image into an embroidery design. It includes several basic photo-editing tools as well as the capability to alter stitch angle, density, and other parameters.

4D Picture Stitch uses one of four methods to create an embroidered representation of a digital image.

CMYK
A color image printed on an inkjet printer combines four ink colors to create shading in the image – Cyan, Magenta, Yellow, and blacK (abbreviated CMYK). 4D Picture Stitch uses the same process and relies upon those four colors of thread to create the shading in an embroidered image/design. Because of the method used to create the design, a 4D Picture Stitch image tends to look best at a distance of 6 – 8 feet or more since the four thread colors begin to blend visually at this minimum distance.

4-Color Sepia
Four shades of brown create shading in the same manner that CMYK photos are processed.

4-Color Custom
Select four custom thread colors. The image is processed the same way as CMYK.

Monochrome
A monochrome image requires only a single thread color. Altering the density and other factors produces image shading. Although we often think of black and white monochrome pictures, thread colors such as deep red, med grey, or tawny brown frequently produce beautiful monochrome Picture Stitch designs.

While both 4D Picture Stitch and 4D Cross Stitch can convert an image or photo into an embroidered design, these modules use a very different method to process the photo, and therefore, each produces a very different result. 4D Cross Stitch uses a pixilated representation of the photo. Digital photos are really a set of dots of different colors that are so close together that they produce a fluid image to our eyes. 4D Cross Stitch uses this concept to divide the image into pixels. Each cross-stitch corresponds to one image pixel. The more pixels (or cross-stitches) are in the picture, the better the representation of the original photo. With 4D Cross Stitch, the shading in the image results from using multiple thread shades (often twelve or more threads). 4D Picture Stitch utilizes only four thread colors for a color image and creates shading by layering these threads over one another in varying stitch densities or by varying the density of a single thread color for a monochrome image.

Because of the method in which 4D Picture Stitch processes an image, editing the initial image, in what would seem to be an unusual way, produces a more attractive embroidery design. The exercise in this chapter demonstrates how to edit an image to increase facial contrast and how to alter stitches to produce an attractive embroidered photo.

EXERCISE 1: "WOMAN'S FACE"

LOAD PICTURE

1. Launch 4D Picture Stitch from 4D Extra .

2. View Picture 📷 and open
   C:\4DEmbroidery\PictureLibrary\
   Photos\People\PEOgenrl\p0322715.jpg

   Since each photo requires unique editing and density settings, an alternate image is not given for this exercise. Study the photo editing, thread density, and contrast techniques demonstrated with the suggested image.

3. To get a very basic idea of how the photo will look, select
   3D Create Stitches ✂. The image processing time depends upon the computing power of your computer and the picture processing settings.

4. Notice the information given such as the size of your embroidery design and the number of stitches. The number of stitches is very important. Typically, work toward a design with approximately 20,000 to 60,000 stitches for the Creative Large Hoop (225 mm x 140mm). Expect more stitches for a larger hoop and fewer for a smaller hoop.

5. Select Cancel since it is not necessary to save this version of the design.

1. Select the Monochrome Linear mode ▤ from the top toolbar. If this option is not visible, select the drop-down arrow just to the left of Contrast ◑ to choose Monochrome Linear.

2. Set Contrast ◑ = 3

3. Scan Depth 〜 = 1

4. Density ▨ = 2

5. Angle ◪ = 335

6. Select Hoop ▢. Hoop Group = Pfaff 2170/2144/2140, Hoop Size = 225mm x 140mm - Creative Large Hoop, Orientation = Vertical, OK to complete the hoop changes.

7. Set Preferences ▦ to Border Width = 4.0mm, Density = 4, Underlay = unchecked, Border Thread color = Robison Anton Rayon 40, color 2484. Monochrome Thread Color = Robison Anton Rayon 40, color 2565. Do not alter the four suggested thread colors. Select OK.

CONVERT TO BLACK AND WHITE AND CROP

This example demonstrates working with a monochrome picture since it is easier to see how contrast and density affect the design produced.

1. On the right hand side of the screen, select Filters = Grayscale and click Apply. This converts the photo to a black and white image.

2. Choose Box Select 🔲 and left click, hold and drag a box around the woman's face. Start just above the bangs in her hair and drag the box just below her chin. Crop ⌗ the image to the selected area.

3. Save the edited photo as Womans Face b and w.

4. Choose 3D Create Stitches 🖊 to see the initial embroidery design. The photo is too dark and the design is too dense. To correct these issues, several changes need to be made. Click Cancel since this design is unacceptable.

ALTER FACIAL CONTRAST

1. From the right hand work area, select Effects→ Brightness

and then Preview. Move the slider bar to 21 and finalize the changes with OK.

2. Increase the contrast by selecting Effects → Contrast and click Preview. Move the slider bar to 10 and choose OK. Once again, choose 3D Create Stitches to see how her face changes slightly with the photo editing. Click Cancel once you have seen the example.

ADD FACIAL HIGHLIGHTS

To accentuate natural facial lines, sometimes it is helpful to add highlights and shadows to the image.

1. Select the dark charcoal colored box on the right side of the screen then select Freehand Draw from the photo editing tools at the left side of the screen.

2. Choose the thinnest line and draw a curved line at the top of each of her eyes. Draw in facial features as shown in the example.

3. Raise the pen off the pen tablet frequently (or release the mouse if you are using one). Use Undo to correct lines. Perfection is definitely not necessary, just the general idea is fine.

4. Using the thin line, draw in zigzag lines for her eyebrows, a line around the nose outline and lines around the mouth area. Using the pen and touchpad set is much easier than a mouse or touchpad for this process.

5. Choose Save Picture As 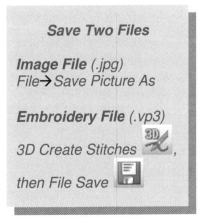 Edited Womans Face.jpg.

6. Select 3D Create Stitches to see how the face changes. Save the embroidery design as edited womans face.vp3.

Save Two Files

Image File *(.jpg)*
File→Save Picture As

Embroidery File *(.vp3)*
3D Create Stitches,
then File Save

REMOVE UNNECESSARY STITCHES

1. Select the 4D Extra tab (at the very bottom of the screen—4D Extra is always open when any other 4D Suite module is in use).

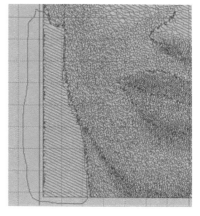

2. Open Edited Womans Face.vp3

3. Select the Edit tab. Zoom In  to the left side of her neck. Use Freehand Select and encircle the unnecessary stitches.

Delete these stitches. Also delete the unneeded stitches at the right side of her face.

4. If necessary, select single stitches and delete or move them. Use the Start and End Draw Ranges to narrow down and work with a specific range of stitches.

5. Save the completed design as Edited Womans Face2.vp3.

Experiment with different monochrome stitches (⊚ spiral,

monochrome mazes 🔲 🔲, etc). Use 3D Create Stitches

✂️ to see how each one alters the design.

Contrast ◐, Scan Depth ᐜ, Density ▨, and Angle

▨ all significantly affect the completed embroidery design. Changing these options is a trial and error process, but it will help to create an attractive embroidery design.

Here is a brief overview of contrast, scan depth and density:

Contrast ◐ - As contrast number increases, dark areas become darker and light areas become lighter. In 4-color modes, contrast ranges from 0–200; in monochrome modes, contrast ranges from 0-100.

Scan Depth ᐜ - Distance between lines or patterns. Lower scan depth produces more detail, and consequently, more stitches. In 4-color modes, scan depth ranges from 1-2; in monochrome modes, scan depth ranges from 1-4.

Density ▨ Lower density number produces more stitches (more dense design). In monochrome and 4-color modes, density ranges from 1-2.

Refer to the 4D Picture Stitch Reference Guide for a more extensive explanation of how to alter these options to produce an attractive design.

- Practice, Practice, Practice! Learning to create an attractive design comes much more from experience than from following specific guidelines.

- Don't be afraid to try changing picture settings, but just as this exercise demonstrated, save each step in the process. That way if the changes are unacceptable, you can go back to the previous picture.

- Contrast and Density are the most important factors in creating a pleasing design.

- Strive for a stitch count of about 20,000 to 60,000 stitches for a 225mm x 140mm hoop (fewer if you are using a smaller hoop, more when using larger hoops).

- Compare the 4D Picture Stitch version of the woman's face with the 4D Cross Stitch version of her face to see how each module processes an image differently.

- Consult Kim Haler's *PictureStitch Techniques: Workbook for the 3D Embroidery Software* for an excellent discussion of picture techniques using PictureStitch.

4D FABRIC DECORATOR

INTRODUCTION

With 4D Fabric Decorator, you can create custom fabric motifs and create beautiful fabric backgrounds from your new motif or from included motif designs.

EXERCISE 1: GOLD LACE

LAUNCH MOTIF WIZARD

1. Launch 4D Fabric Decorator ⭐ from 4D Extra. The 4D Fabric Decorator Wizard opens.

2. Select Create Fabric, and check the box entitled "Always show motif wizard on startup." Select Next.

The next window shows numerous motif options. Working with motifs in 4D Fabric Decorator is very similar to working with motifs in other 4D modules.

Scroll through several of the motifs and notice that each motif has a standard size (in mm) and that each one is unique. The default size is normally the size of that stitch on the sewing machine since many of the motifs are, in fact, machine stitches. The height and width of the motif varies within a range limit which is specific to each motif. Consider this size range in comparison with the area to be filled. For example, a small area might look best with a small motif while a larger area might accommodate a larger motif.

1. Select Motif 1 = Pfaff→Cross Stitches→stitch # 7

   ⬛🔲🔲🔲 7 ⬛, Height = 9mm, Width = 36mm, Proportional = checked, Reverse = unchecked, Mirror = unchecked.

2. Check the Use Motif 2 box.

3. Select Motif 2 = Pfaff→Cross Stitches→stitch # 6

   🔲🔲🔲 6 ⬛, Height = 8.1mm, Width = 18.1mm, Proportional = checked, Reverse = unchecked, Mirror = unchecked

4. Other option settings: Center Motifs 1 and 2 = unchecked, Standard Repeat = unchecked, Gap: Horizontal % = 0, Vertical % = 0, Offset: Horizontal % = 0, Vertical % = 0.

5. Click Motif Options. Select Angle = 30, Running Stitch, Length = 2.0mm. *The new motif angle will not be visible until the final step of the Wizard.* Choose OK, then Next.

6. Select Change Hoop and set Hoop Group = Pfaff Creative Vision, Hoop Size = 360mm x 200mm – creative Deluxe Hoop, Orientation = Horizontal, OK to continue.

7. Fabric Area Shape = Rectangle, Proportional = unchecked.

8. Select the Output thread color as Robison Anton Metallic J 40, color 1000 (gold).

9. Check the Add Border box. Width = 3.0mm, Density = 4, Underlay box = checked, Border thread color = Robison Anton Metallic J 40, color = 1013 (black).

10. Check the box Make as Appliqué. Set running and double stitch lengths = 2.0, Method = second box (bottom).

11. Select Next.

1. The Export Options window shows the final design, including the 30° stitch angle, and indicates the dimensions of the new design.

2. Preview the design in Real Size .

3. Select Save Fabric as Design Outline (.can) File and save the file as Gold Lace.can in the My Designs folder.

4. Save Fabric as an Embroidery File 🖫 under the name Gold Lace.vp3.

5. Select Finish to close the Fabric Wizard. Open Gold Lace.vp3 in 4D Organizer or 4D Extra to view the embroidery design.

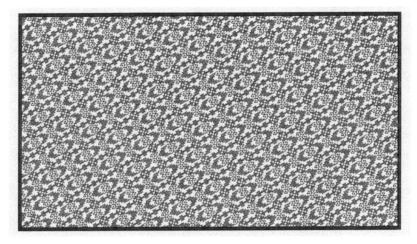

The lace color in this example picture is RA Metallic J 40 color 1009.

EXERCISE 2: "FLOATING HEARTS"

SELECT PICTURE FOR NEW MOTIF

A motif created in 4D Fabric Decorator, and saved in the ".mot"
file format, may be used in other 4D software modules.

1. Click on New (File) 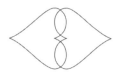 to begin the Fabric Wizard.

2. Select Create New Motif and then Next.

3. View Picture and browse to
   open the file:
   C:\4DEmbroidery\Samples\4DEmb\
   Pics2\Motifs\1CMo13.png, then Next.

4. It is not necessary to rotate the picture, so choose Next
   again.

5. Move the Monochrome Threshold slider bar to 127.
   Select Next.

6. The cropped area is already selected correctly, so select
   Next again.

7. Set Height = 20 mm.

8. Check the Use Auto Trace box and
   the Quick Trace Heavy button.
   Select Finish.

1. Select Preferences  from the top toolbar. On the Screen tab, check the 3D View Orientation = Horizontal button and set the number of motifs = 5. Grid Size = 3.0mm and the 3D Display and Tablet Input buttons are checked. Select OK.

2. Zoom In ⌕ to the area surrounding the last stitch in the motif.

   Last Stitch

3. Click on the last stitch to place a selection box around it (indicated by an "X").

   Add Candlewicking Here

4. From the right-hand toolbar, select the Candlewicking icon ✴.

5. Tap the next grid point to the right of the last stitch.

6. The Candlewick Options window opens. Set Type = Star, Ties = 3, Star Options: Points = 9, Width = 5.0mm, Height = 5.0mm. OK.

7. Right click to deselect the Candlewicking tool.

8. Zoom to Fit ✴.

9. Save 💾 the motif in the My Designs folder as Floating Heart.mot.

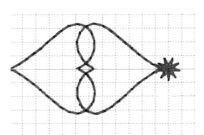

10. Select Export to MyMotifs 📥 from the top toolbar.

1. Choose Create Fabric 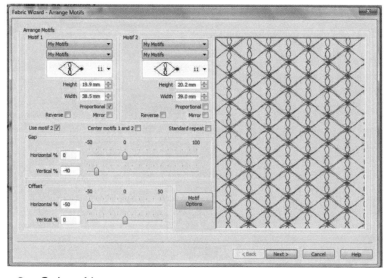 from the top toolbar. The Fabric Wizard opens and automatically selects the new motif.

2. The Arrange Motifs window options are: Motif 1 – Height = 19.9 mm, check the Proportional box. Check Use Motif 2. Motif 2 options are: Height = 20.2 mm, Height = 39.0mm, Proportional box = unchecked. Gap: Horizontal % = 0, Vertical % = -40. Offset: Horizontal % = -50, Vertical % = 0.

3. Select Next.

4. Select Hoop = Pfaff Creative Vision, 360mm x 200mm creative Deluxe Hoop, Horizontal orientation. OK.

5. Fabric Shape Area = Ellipse, Proportional = unchecked.

6. Change Output Thread Color to Robison-Anton Rayon Vari 40, color 2344. OK.

7. Border: Add Border = checked, Width = 3.0 mm, Density = 5, Underlay = checked. Change the border thread color to Robison-Anton Metallic J 40, color 1005. OK.

8. Make as Appliqué = checked, Method = Running Stitch-Stop-Fabric-Stop-Double Stitch-Stop-Satin (second box), Running Stitch Length = 3.0, Double Stitch Length = 2.0.

   When the machine embroiders the appliqué, it begins with a single running stitch, indicating where to place the appliqué fabric. The machine stops so you can insert the appliqué fabric. The second "color block" is a double stitched tacking stitch. Pull the hoop out of the machine and trim carefully around the appliquéd fabric. Place the hoop back into the machine and sew the final color block—the satin border around the appliqué. If you prefer to skip the first running stitch (because you already know where the appliqué will be placed), simply advance the machine to the second thread color block.

9. Select Next. Save the Fabric as an Embroidery file in the MyDesigns folder as Oval Floating Hearts.vp3. Then Save Fabric as a Design Outline (.can) file with the same name (Oval Floating Hearts.can).

10. Print a worksheet 🖨 for reference.

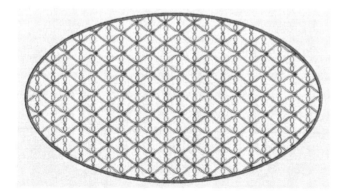

- Add motifs to the work area by selecting Insert Motif from the top toolbar.

- Since motifs are created from image files (most formats such as .bmp, .jpeg, etc are supported), a piece of clip art or a scanned line design could be used to create a motif. Images with strong, clear lines will produce the best motifs.

- Consider using an Endless Hoop. Create a full piece of fabric with an embroidered motif over the entire piece of fabric. Think of how lovely this would be on a jacket, skirt, or vest—very much like many ready-made garments that are popular now, but with your custom design!

INTRODUCTION

With 4D Stitch Artist, you can create new 9mm or maxi stitches (not embroidery designs). 4D Stitch Artist is ideal for creating custom "crazy patch" stitches.

EXERCISE 1: "CRESCENT" MAXI STITCH

CREATE MAXI STITCH

1. Launch 4D Stitch Artist from 4D Extra by selecting Quicklink→Accessories→4D Stitch Artist. (It does not have a launch icon).

2. The Design Wizard opens automatically when the program is started (it can also be started by clicking the New file icon from the top toolbar). Choose Maxi and then Next.

3. Select View Picture and open the file C:\4DEmbroidery\Samples\4DEmb\Pics2\Fashion\ 1CFa25.png. Click Next. Click Next again to step past the Rotate picture window.

4. Adjust Monochrome Threshold until the preview window shows only the outline of the design (approximately 74 on the slider bar).

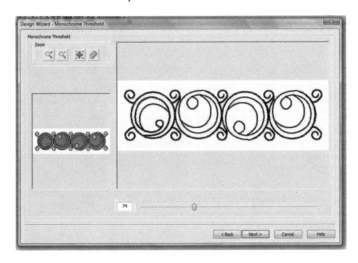

5. Select Next and Next again when the Crop Picture window appears.

6. Picture Height = 42 mm, Auto Trace = checked, Quick Trace Heavy = checked. Select Finish. The Design Information suggests foot number 8 with tension = 4.0.

Add any notes you wish to make about this stitch, Apply and then close the window.

7. Save the file [icon] as Crescent.spx for the Pfaff Creative Vision or Crescent.max for the 2140/2144/2170 machine series. (The Creative Vision also reads .max files.)

VIEW STITCH IN 3D AND REAL SIZE

1. Select Preferences ▤. On the Screen tab, Orientation = Horizontal, Stitches = 3, Grid Size = 3.0. Click OK.

2. Choose 3D Realistic Mode 🔲 from the top toolbar to preview the new stitch. View the stitch in Real Size 📐 and then click Cancel to close the preview window.

ALTER STITCH COLOR

1. Select Set Stitch Color 🔵 from the top toolbar. Choose Sulky Poly Neon 40, color = 1910.

ADDITIONAL FEATURES

Create Maxi or 9 mm stitches using 4D Stitch Artist. In the Design Wizard, simply select the preferred stitch type.

Notice that several of the right-hand toolbar icons are similar to those available in the 4D Design Creator and 4D Fabric Decorator modules. Create light 🌷 and heavy 🌷 traces, satin stitches (curved ▤, columns ▥ and fixed angle ◣), and single ✏, running ◩, triple ◩ and candlewicking ✳ freehand stitches.

4D DESIGN ALIGNER

INTRODUCTION

With 4D Design Aligner, you can divide a large design into sections to stitch it in any hoop size.

EXERCISE 1: SPLIT A LARGE FLOWER

OPEN DESIGN

1. Launch 4D Design Aligner 🌐 from 4D Extra.
2. Change Hoop to Hoop Group = Pfaff 2170/2144/2140, Hoop Size = 120mm x 115mm – creative Rectangular Hoop, Orientation = Vertical. OK.
3. Overlap = 20mm, Alignment Stitch Style = Corner, Compensation = None. Next.
4. View Embroidery 📷 and open the file C:\4DEmbroidery\Samples\4DEmb\ Stitch2\Flowers\FlowersLarge.vp3. Finish.

PREPARE TO SPLIT DESIGN

This design will require three hoop changes to fit into the Rectangular Hoop. 4D Design Aligner indicates the overlap area between the three hoopings (shown in white) and suggests where the design should be split (along the black lines with square dots). The black squares along the split lines are moveable split points.

We specified a 20mm overlap between each hoop split, so this will be the maximum movement of the split line.

1. Zoom in  to the flower area in the top split.

2. Notice that this design has a natural split between the round flower and the middle region. This will be an ideal location to divide the design.

3. Move the three middle squares so that they are between the top flower and the center region.

Move these three points.

4. Zoom to Fit 🔲. Then Zoom In 🔍 to view the lower split region. Move three points to split this area similarly.

SPLIT DESIGN INTO SECTIONS

1. Split the Design 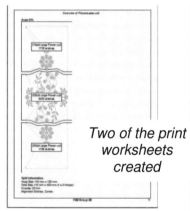.

2. 4D Design Creator indicates that the design is being split and opens preview windows showing the three sections.

    Select ▶ to cycle through each of the three parts of the design.

3. Save 💾 the file as Split Large Flower.vp3.

PREVIEW AND PRINT SECTIONS

1. Choose File→Print Preview to see the print worksheets created by 4D Design Aligner.

2. Select Next Page or Previous Page to browse through the informational printouts that are available. Notice that each portion of the design has a unique name: 01Split Large Flower.vp3, 02 Split Large Flower.vp3, and 03Split Large Flower.vp3.

3. If desired, Print the worksheets.

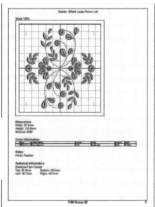

Two of the print worksheets created

HOW TO STITCH A SPLIT DESIGN

- Alignment stitches are sewn at the beginning of a design. After sewing the first design section, use precise positioning (or precise rotational positioning on the Creative Vision or 2170 series machines) to position the starting alignment stitches of the second design over the ending alignment stitches from the first design.
- Consider printing worksheets (or selected worksheet pages) on vellum to create a template for alignment. On a particularly precise design, this is very helpful. The design created in this exercise is not an overly precise split since the design already had an open space between the portions of the original design.

WHERE TO SPLIT A DESIGN

- Look for designs with small open spaces between portions of the design. These are the easiest and least noticeable areas to split a design.
- Try to match the size of the expected design parts with the size of the hoop.
- If necessary, make the overlap area larger to accommodate a particularly precise split.
- When the design cannot be split in an open area, split satin stitches parallel to the satin stitch direction so that the next design portion will cover the first.
- In particularly difficult areas where the split will be difficult to cover, consider using 4D Extra, 4D Design Creator or 4D Sketch to add additional cover stitches in the second design portion.
- If necessary, Insert 🔧 or Delete 🔧 split points.

4D FONT DIGITIZING

INTRODUCTION

4D Font Digitizing is an accessory module. To launch it from any of the 4D software modules, select the small arrow adjacent to Accessories and choose 4D Font Digitizing. Although 4D QuickFont, the 4D QuickFont Wizard (4D Embroidery Extra, Letters

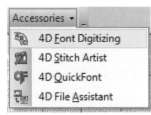

tab), and 4D Font Digitizing each create new embroidery fonts, there are important differences between 4D QuickFont and 4D Font Digitizing. [*4D QuickFont and the 4D QuickFont Wizard are very similar, and for this discussion, they will be collectively referred to as 4D QuickFont*]. Here are some of the significant differences between the two:

	4D QuickFont	4D Font Digitizing
Creates all characters in font set	Yes automatically	One at a time manually
Digitize one character at a time	No	Yes
Edit individual characters in font	No	Yes
Limited to TrueType or OpenType fonts	Yes	Use any font or picture
Control over font characteristics	Limited	Full
Creates font automatically	Yes	No
Digitize font by hand/freehand	No	Yes
Edit built-in 4D Extra fonts	No	Yes
Edit built-in 4D Extra shapes	No	Yes
Create new shape set	No	Yes
Time to create new font set	Few minutes	Lengthy
Experience level	Beginner	Intermediate to Advanced

Here are some of the features offered by 4D Font Digitizing:

- Create your own custom font or shape with extensive control over font and shape characteristics.
- Prepare new fonts and shapes or edit existing fonts and shapes. It is often helpful to use 4D QuickFont to prepare a new font set automatically. Then import the font set into 4D Font Digitizing to edit individual characters and add custom touches to the new font.
- Use a background image as a guide for the new font or shape.
- Insert design files (.can) created in 4D Design Creator.
- Insert any of the following commands: Color Change , Stop Command , Jump Stitch , Tie Off , Single Stitch .
- Add freehand design elements including: Straight Column , Curved Column , Fill , Hole , Fill + Border , Border , Running Stitch line , Double Stitch line , Triple Stitch line . *Notice that these are similar to the freehand digitizing tools found in 4D Design Creator.*
- Insert and Delete objects or Insert and Delete points.
- Choose from Uniform or Non-Uniform font properties (change characteristics of all characters or shapes in the set or change preferences for each one individually).

Important concepts to understand when working with 4D Font Digitizing:

- Critical: If you edit a built-in 4D font or shape (those included when you first install the 4D software), it will be permanently changed. It is much safer to create a font in 4D QuickFont and edit only these fonts. Save edited fonts in the MyFonts category.
- Each character is digitized separately. Start with the capital "A." You must create at least four characters in a new font set.
- Since it is often time consuming to create an entire font set, Save, Save, Save! Plan to save your work frequently and consider saving changes under different filenames so you can revert to previous file versions if necessary (i.e. save the initial font as fontABC.nft, then save changes under the name fontABC_2.nft).
- The work area is shown in 2D. To view a 3-dimensional image of the embroidered font, choose 3D Create Stitches .
- Insert four points to add a Satin Column :

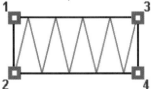

- Insert eight points to add a Curved Column :

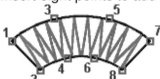

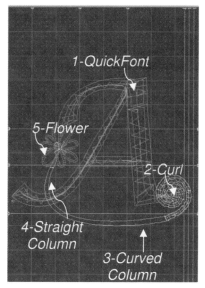

Example project:

Use 4D Extra QuickFont Wizard to create new font: Lucida Calligraphy (Reg, Satin, 20-50mm).

Use 4D Extra to edit and extract parts of existing designs (Flower and Curl).

Import Flower and Curl designs into 4D Design Creator and save as .can (design) files.

In 4D Font Digitizing, Start with Existing Font (Lucida Calligraphy). Work with the "A" character. Add Color Change to pewter metallic thread

and then Insert the Design Curl.can. Place curl at lower

right corner of "A." Insert a Curved Column with eight points defining the curve. Start at the curl and end just below where the flower will be added. Add four points to define a

Straight Column ▦ with a point on the upper edge. Insert

Color Change ◕ to mauve metallic thread and Insert the

Design 📷 Flower.can. 3D Generate Stitches

✂ to view the embroidered design.

File→Save As 💾 LucidaCalligraphy2.nft.

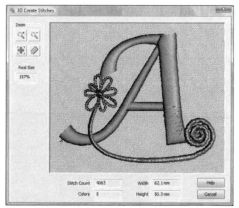

Software Solutions: Introduction to 4D Embroidery Suite is designed as a workbook for either independent study or classroom instruction. This section of the book provides resource material for teachers who plan to use the workbook in a classroom setting.

RECOMMENDED CLASSROOM SUPPLIES

- High-resolution projector and projection screen connected to the teacher's laptop computer
- One computer for each student
- One copy of the workbook for each student and pencils or pens for making notes during class
- Embroidered samples of software projects
- Pfaff embroidery machine(s) connected to the teacher's laptop to demonstrate how to send a design from the computer to the machine

RECOMMENDED TEACHER PREPARATION

- Attend Pfaff 4D software certification classes and continuing education seminars.
- Work through all workbook exercises several times to become thoroughly familiar with each project.
- Make notes of questions that students ask in class so you can answer these questions in the next session or in future classes.
- Regularly spend time working with the 4D software.

SUGGESTED CLASS SCHEDULES

OPTION 1: TWO-DAY SEMINAR

- Day 1: (5 - 6 Hours)
  4D Design Creator, 4D Cross Stitcher, 4D Stitch Editor, 4D Sketch

- Day 2: (6 hours)
  4D Picture Stitch, 4D Fabric Decorator, 4D Stitch Artist, 4D Design Aligner, 4D Font Digitizing

OPTION 2: THREE 4-HOUR CLASSES

- Session 1: 4D Design Creator, 4D Cross Stitcher, 4D Stitch Editor
- Session 2: 4D Sketch, 4D Picture Stitch
- Session 3: 4D Fabric Decorator, 4D Stitch Artist, 4D Design Aligner, 4D Font Digitizing

OPTION 3: SOFTWARE CLUB

- Cover individual modules separately, approximately 1 – 1 ½ hours per session.

❖ When *Software Solutions: Introduction to 4D Suite* is taught in a classroom setting, each student must purchase a book. Copyright laws prohibit copying pages of the book.

www.learn4D.com

LSA54